Staying Happy & Confident When Your World Is Falling Apart

Written by

Seifuddin Henton

Dedication

I've assisted many people with unlocking their greatness. Now I get to do it for the world. I wish everyone success, peace, and happiness.

This book is dedicated to everyone around the world who are in their own struggle. Whether mentally or physically, this is for you. Just stay strong, hold on, and the journey will get better as time goes on. Your mind is stronger than you know. We live our lives 100% in our mind. Our thoughts control our world. More specifically, our thoughts ARE our world. Feed your thoughts with joy and endless possibilities. Much love, much success, peace & happiness to you.

Contents

1. Bio   6
2. Attracting Money   10
3. We Never Fail!!!   14
4. Happiness & Confidence   18
5. Everything Happens for a Reason - Some Depression is Healthy   20
6. Pump Fake Your Feelings   23
7. Never Settle for Less.   27
8. Think Big!   30
9. Daily Pickups   32

1
Bio

I was born with a success mindset. I was always extremely observant. I only knew success. Since the age of 6, in 1st grade, I envisioned having access to everything I ever wanted in life. I'm talking about obtaining a nice house, not too big, a wife, and some children. I planned to achieve this all while working from home. I also visualized cars, a helipad and helicopter, a maid, and a butler. Let's not forget athletic aspects, like a basketball court, a track, a tennis court, a boxing ring and whatever else I wanted without having to leave my property.

My actual living situation was extremely far from my vision. It included living in homeless shelters as a child and wearing my dad's old clothing as a teenager. I always felt as if I were living someone else's life. I was, simply, working daily to live the life I envisioned. Thankfully, I was born with two gifts. One was the ability to have extreme focus in all situations. The other was the mindset to simplify every situation into a big game.

These gifts helped shape the road to a great journey.

I am the oldest of my mother's eight children and the fourth born of my dad's eleven children. Even though I came from a family of Real Estate investors, but it wasn't the go to business for the family. Life wasn't easy for us at all. My maternal great-grandparents came to New York City from Jamaica. They had 16 children & brought at least one house for each of them. They paid for in the properties in full, with cash, no mortgages. Many investment properties were brought. My great aunt even owned an entire town in Boston, which consisted of mostly livestock. When the elders died, so did most of the investing. Very few continued to have the vision of real estate investing. It's similar to children who inherit their family business, many don't carry on the business.

We didn't have it so easy growing up. However, no matter what, our parents instilled in us that we can achieve whatever we put our minds to. My mom kept the real estate investing alive by telling me stories of past and present family members in the real estate game.

My dad was a natural visionary, entrepreneur, chess master, mathematician, and philanthropist. He devoted his life to enhancing his community. We were very close. He taught me how to be a man, how to play chess and to care for others. He told me to do things the smart way, not the hard way. He insisted I use tools to my advantage. I was in 11th grade when he became ill and died of cancer.

I planned my life from since elementary school. I meditated before I knew what it was. School was a twelve year prison sentence for me. My goal was to do everything in my power to graduate without getting held back. I remember staring out the window at the skyscrapers, waiting for the day I'd own a few. In school we were taught to be blind followers. For example, on tests, if you get an answer correct but fail to give the correct formula, the teacher would still mark it wrong. So in other words, if you did not use the school's formula, the answer was wrong. To me, this was Brainwashing the children to diminish their creativity & problem solving skills. Those skills are necessary to be successful in business and life. "C" students are the visionary people. Which is why "C" students employ "A" & "B" students.

Notes:

2

Attracting Money

A financier/ mentor told me, "Seifuddin, if you don't learn how to create money out of thin air, you will never have money."

When it comes to making money, you must align yourself with people who are much more successful than you in the field you seek to achieve in.

Learn from them. Ask questions, and more questions, until you fully understand. If they have an issue with you asking them questions, they are not the mentor for you. Learn from the mistakes of your mentors. Learn what brought them great success. This will save you decades of despair. Learn how you can be of value to them as well. Every successful person knows what he or she needs in order to move to the next level. They'll tell you what they need solved. These are opportunistic problems you can solve for them. This can be very lucrative, and usually will be life changing for you, simply, if you decide to put in the work to solve his or her problems.

How to make $1,000,000

Sell a $200 Product to 5,000 People.

Sell a $500 Product to 2,000 People.

Sell a $1,000 Product to 1000 People.

Sell a $2,000 Product to 250 People.

Sell a $1M Product to 1 person.

Subscriptions

5,000 People Pay $17/ month, For 12 months.

2,000 People Pay $42/ month, For 12 months.

1,000 People Pay $83/ month, For 12 months.

500 People Pay $167/ month, For 12 months.

250 People Pay $333/ month, For 12 months.

Keep that chart in mind when creating money

3 Keys to a happy successful business life

1. What's your passion? What would you be doing if you didn't have to think about money?

2. How does your passion solve problems? The bigger the problems, the bigger the money potential.

3. When the economy drops, will you still have a successful business? Will your business still be efficient?

Have those 3 things in place, & you'll have a fighting chance at extreme success, financially.

Notes:

3
We never fail!!!

We don't fail. We weren't handed the blueprint or formula to life. We are scientists! We have a hypothesis & then we experiment. Based on the results of the experiment, we develop a new hypothesis. As time goes on we learn what works and what doesn't. There is no right or wrong, only causes and effects. Want a different result? Keep tweaking it until you get it. Keep it simple.

Stop setting time limits for goals. We never complete them in the exact time frame we set anyway. Time is an illusion. Instead focus on what you can control. We never know what we need to experience, or who we need to meet, in order to achieve what we seek to achieve. They never say "This scientist finally achieved this after 30 years of failing." Instead, scientists are glorified for their inventions.

Never focus on the, so called, accomplishments of other people, especially peers and family members. We all have our own journeys and our own paths. What may work for someone else may not work out for you, and vice versa. Never allow others to compare your journey to another's, especially family. Many people aren't happy with their own lives. How can you allow them to criticize yours?

Don't dwell wishing you knew the things you know now. Nor should you wish you got started while younger. Live now! Do now! Go after it now! Assist the younger generations with the information you wish you had at their ages. Become a mentor.

Keys to success:

#1. Must go 100% all in.

#2. Stay focused.

#3. Stay persistent.

#4. Never settle for less, EVER.

#5. Take advantage of opportunities.

Bonus: Get a mentor.

Seek out and learn from people who are successful in the field you seek to be successful in.

Notes:

4
Happiness and Confidence

Become the most positive and enthusiastic person you know. Happiness and confidence go hand and hand. Continuous, or near permanent, happiness often comes from working towards something that you enjoy.

Life is a game. Treat it as such. You must know you are bigger than every situation that comes your way.

Never get too attached to things. Always know you have the ability to attract better. You have the power over the things you possess, not the other way around. This goes for everything! Such as clothing, furniture, cars, houses, jobs, businesses, and, even, people or relationships. Everything is replaceable, and usually is replaced in life. In many cases, this also goes for people. Know that your worth is greater than any situation you are in. Never settle for less, ever. Move on.

At any moment we can lose both things and people (in the physical form).

3 Keys to having peace and happiness:

1. Have zero expectations.
2. Never settle for less, ever.
3. Appreciate everything.

Notes:

5
Everything happens for a reason. Some depression is healthy.

Think about the most catastrophic things that has happened in your life in the past. You were victorious 100% of the time!!! You will have the same outcome with this situation. Life simply goes on. Even the human body will heal itself if you allow it to.

Write down all the things you love about yourself. Write all the things you're proud of and all the things you've accomplished. Keep it with you at all times.

Before something great happens, something perceived as bad usually happens. You have to let the old go in order to receive the new. A closed fist doesn't receive, you have to open it.

Find the opportunity in every situation. You have the ability to find several ways out of every situation you encounter.

If used properly, depression can be an excellent tool to groundbreaking achievements.

This is in both individual lives and within general economics. Research the Great Depression and each time there was a recession. These are the times that create the most millionaires.

You are still, for the first time in a long time. Use the calmness to your advantage. Use it to regroup. Use it to research successful people and their stories. Chances are they'll match your current situation. Listen to the soothing or motivational music of your choice. Let go and go to sleep.

If you have to force it, it doesn't fit. Let it go. You can do better and receive better. You will attract better if you only settle for the best.

Notes:

6
Pump fake your feelings.

Feed your subconscious daily.

I ONLY care about success. Tell yourself at least five times a day "I love me", "I love my mind", "I love my life". Eventually it'll become true & real. Only watch funny and motivational movies, especially if it's about success.

Change your screensaver to your vision of success. Change your ringtones to reflect what you want.

Example: I needed money deals to call my phone. So I changed it to Juelz Santana "Hold on I got that money calling on the other line. My phone clicking, my phone clicking." Eventually money literally started calling me. My phone became my only source of income.

Stop watching the news!!!!!!

ONLY follow pages, profiles, and people that are positive on social media. Put hashtags like success, happiness, etc in the search. After finding someone to follow, check to see how consistent the person is who posted it. If they have a consistent uploading pattern, follow them. Immediately, when you look on your social media, you will mostly see positivity. You will be able to look at your phone and feel motivated! This is especially important for starting your day feeling excellent!

Share these posts as well, while giving recognition to the origin.

Unfollow all people who don't post positive things.

Don't talk ill of people. Refuse to accept such thinking around you.

There is no good or bad. Only causes and effects. Hedge every situation as often as possible. Only give what you don't expect to receive back. This goes to all forms of energy. Both in personal and business life, including investments.

Don't be afraid to let go. There is no such thing as starting over. We bring the experience along with us. Remember, energy never dies, it simply transfers from one form to another.

Stay away from everything that doesn't bring you peace and happiness. Especially people, including family. Don't argue. Stop caring so much. Simply say "ok," then, keep it moving. Say "I love you, see you later." Keep the power! Assume the blame and keep it moving.

At all costs, if the energy doesn't feel right, don't go. Don't join.

Notes:

7
Never settle for less!!!

Know exactly what you want in life. This includes attributes in your spouse, the amount of children, your occupation, the size of your house, the type of car, your sexual desires, how you want your food, how you want to be treated, and how you need to be supported mentally, physically, & emotionally. Go on that vacation you always wanted. Treat yourself at least once a month to a movie, nice restaurant, and spa.

State EXACTLY what you want & don't settle for less. Then go 100% after it.

Write down your vision. I wrote my wealthy checklist when I was 17 & 18 years old. I had a big copy on my wall over my bed. Every time I woke up, I saw it. Every time I went to sleep, I saw it. I kept a mini note pad with the same wealthy checklist in my pocket. I never said this is what I want to do, or would like to do. I said I'm 100% doing it!!! People asked me how would I make it happen. I said "I don't know, don't care, just know I'm doing it!!!!"

I never use phrases like "I'll try," "same stuff different day," "just trying to keep my head above water," (in other words you're almost drowning!!!) Stay away from low frequencies & vibrations.

Know you are an eagle!!!! You have the ability to fly above the clouds! Don't be a chicken or an ostrich sticking your head in the ground when pressured.

Notes:

8
Think Big!!!

Everything is an illusion. Life is a game. We are all fragments of our imagination. Life is literally how we view it. We have good or bad days based on our feelings. Once you truly grasp this idea, you can play with your own emotions. Shift them to your liking, like changing the channel on the TV.

Two people can have gone to the same vacation together. Did the same activities, but when asked how it went for each person, they may have night and day experiences.

When it all balls down to it, stop caring about what people think, and do exactly what brings you joy, peace, and happiness.

Notes:

9
Daily Pickups

- I love me!
- I love my mind!
- I love my life!
- I am me!
- I am great!
- I am the man!
- I am the woman!
- I am bigger than any situation that comes my way!
- There is no item that controls my life!
- There is no one that controls my life!
- I control my life!

- I choose to win!
- All I know is success!
- All I do is win!
- Success no matter what!
- Oh well, life goes on.
- It'll pass.
- I'll live.
- This (insert item or person) doesn't run my life!
- This (thing or person) isn't in charge of my happiness!
- I'm good, regardless.
- I'm the man/ woman!
- This happened so I can receive much better.

Write down,(in this book), all the things you love about yourself. All the things you're proud of. All the things you've accomplished. Keep it with you at all times.

Most importantly...

Everything happens for a much better reason.

It'll be alright.

Thank you for reading this book.

Please share this book with 10 other people.

Together we will enhance the world!

Much continued success, peace, & happiness to you.

Notes:

Notes:

Notes:

www.ingramcontent.com/pod-product-compliance
Lightning Source LLC
Chambersburg PA
CBHW031244160426
43195CB00009BA/593